BIKING TO WORK

Biking to Work

Rory McMullan

Chelsea Green Publishing Company

First published in 2007 by Green Books as *Cycling to Work*

Foxhole, Dartington
Totnes, Devon TQ9 6EB, UK

First Chelsea Green printing January, 2008

Interior design concept by Julie Martin jmartin1@btinternet.com

Photos were kindly supplied by (and are the copyright of): Raleigh, Paul
McMullan / Channel News Service, Nick Turner / Sustrans, J Bewley /
Sustrans, Pfizer, Moore Large, Marin, Powacycle, Madison, Sturmey, and
www.urban75.com.

Printed in Canada.

Text printed on 100-percent postconsumer-waste recycled paper.

10 9 8 7 6 5 4 3 2 1   08 09 10

DISCLAIMER: The advice in this book is believed to be correct at the time
of printing, but the authors and publishers accept no liability for actions
inspired by this book.

Library of Congress Cataloging-in-Publication Data
McMullan, Rory, 1970-
  Biking to work / Rory McMullan.
      p. cm.
  Includes index.
  1. Bicycle commuting--Great Britain. 2. Bicycles. I. Title.

  HE5739.G7M36 2008
  388.3'4720941--dc22

2007046516

Chelsea Green Publishing Company
P.O. Box 428
White River Junction, VT 05001
(802) 295-6300
www.chelseagreen.com

Contents

Acknowledgments

There are a multitude of good reasons to get back on your bike, and fortunately there are plenty of organizations and individuals who work tirelessly to encourage more people to do what is good for them, good for society, and good for the planet.

This book is dedicated to these people, for without their efforts, facilities for cyclists would be nowhere near as good.

Many of these bicycle advocates provided their help, advice, and support in publishing this handbook.

Particular thanks to Carlton Reid, Bikeforall.net; Nick Harvey, BikeWeek; Paul McMullan, Channel News and Pictures; Dave Holladay, CTC; David Dansky, Cycle Training UK; James Steward, Cyclepods; Dolly Sura and Denis Canning, GlaxoSmithKline; Claire Fleming, Nottinghamshire County Council; John Gough and James Graham, Pfizer UK; Michael Hartley, T-Mobile; Mike Sloecome, Urban75.com; Shane Collins, Urban Green Fair; and special thanks to the contributors of case studies. Thanks are also due to the following organizations: Association for Commuter Transport, ATB Sales, Bikemagic.com, CTC, Cycling England, Discount Bicycles, Leeds City Council, London Cycling Campaign, Powacycle, Raleigh Bicycles, SheCycles.com, Stratton Cycles, and Wiltshire County Council.

And finally, a huge thank-you to Jon Clift, Amanda Cuthbert, and John Elford and all of the Green Books team, who did virtually all the work on this book.

Chapter 1

WHY BIKE?

If you are thinking "I can't bike, I live too far from work, I don't want to breathe polluted air, I'm too old, I don't want to get hot and sweaty, I'm unfit . . ." this book just might change your mind.

You're better off by bike!

Biking keeps you healthy and makes you feel better

Regular exercise helps people feel better; studies show that cyclists are absent fewer days and are more productive at work. On average, regular cyclists:

- add over 2 years to their life expectancy
- have the general fitness and health of someone 10 years younger
- are 50% less likely to experience depression

Doctors advise a minimum of 30 minutes moderate exercise a day to keep fit; if you feel unfit, start slowly and work your way up to longer journeys—you will soon gain confidence and fitness. Don't drive to the gym—bike to work!

Biking means a less polluted journey

Research shows that car occupants are exposed to 2–3 times the level of pollution of cyclists.

Cyclists ride up above the most polluted air. Car traffic produces a cocktail of noxious gases that are linked to cancer and respiratory diseases, and you are actually most at risk from air pollution when driving in heavy traffic, as the ventilation system sucks in the emissions from the exhaust of the vehicle in front.

Biking helps you lose weight

Although our calorie intake has hardly risen in the past 30 years, over 60% of us are either overweight or obese; this is almost entirely due to reduced levels of exercise, which have fallen dramatically with the rise in car use and the parallel fall in walking and bike riding.

Losing weight is often seen as the best way to improve self-confidence, whereas fad diets often only work in the short term; cycling not only burns the calories—it is also good for your health and general sense of well-being.

> Biking at a moderate pace of about 10 miles per hour burns on average 400 calories per hour for women and 450 per hour for men—about the same as an aerobics session.

Biking saves you money

The AAA estimates that the average car costs 52¢ per mile to run; and cyclists don't need to feed parking meters or pay to park in a garage or parking lot.

Compare the costs of running a car or monthly parking fees with the $500 it costs to buy a good-quality bike and equipment, which will last you three or more years; you can easily see how much money biking to work will save you, even if you only use your bike for part of the journey.

You don't have to sell the car to start cycling (most regular cyclists are also motorists), but a bike can often replace one car in a two-car family. If you live in a major city with good public transportation you might not need a car at all, as a bicycle can be faster and more convenient.

Biking is quicker and offers more flexibility

Cyclists are the most punctual of all employees: traffic jams do not affect them, neither do train delays. Even if you don't get snarled up in a traffic jam, parking a car can be a nightmare, whereas a bicycle can usually be parked right outside your workplace.

Speed and reliability are the reasons why urgent deliveries are made by bicycle messengers in the world's busiest cities.

> The roads of major cities and towns are almost at gridlock during rush hour; average speeds have hardly risen since 1900, and in some cases have fallen. Because a bicycle is incredibly space-efficient, if we can convert unnecessary car trips to bike trips, then our congestion levels will fall.

Biking is cool

Over the past 50 years riding a bicycle has received bad press: it was the forgotten mode of transportation, the car was king, everybody who didn't have a car was perceived to be poor, and people felt defined by the car they drove. But things are changing; these days mobile phones, Blackberrys, and iPods are the most important accessories for the image-conscious, and biking is becoming part of this new fashion. Cycling, and the healthy, environmentally friendly lifestyle it represents, is now used to advertise mobile phones, laptops, cameras, and, ironically, cars.

Boasting about how quickly you get to work takes on a whole new dimension when you ride a bike. Cyclists spend less on transportation but on average earn more than the average income;

a typical cyclist is a rich, healthy, image-conscious professional; no wonder that high-profile politicians and presidents of global corporations want to be seen biking to work.

Biking is enjoyable

Biking can beat driving for pure enjoyment; in the past few years local authorities in many urban areas have invested heavily in bicycle lanes, many of which go through lovely areas like parks, or along rivers.

THE WIDER PICTURE

Biking helps to combat climate change

Transportation accounts for over 20% of CO_2 emissions, more than half of which comes from private cars.

Many scientific studies have shown global warming and climate change to be real, and it is now fully accepted by governments worldwide that we have a pressing problem. The Stern Report, commissioned by Britain's Treasury Department, estimates that we have to cut our emissions by 60% in the next 30 years to save us from the worst consequences of climate change. Biking to work is not going to solve climate change on its own, but it is part of the solution.

Global warming and the end of the oil age are challenges of immense proportions, but we can help to solve these huge problems by making many small changes in the way we live. We have to start making these changes now; biking more and driving less is one of the easiest and most enjoyable.

Our cities

There is no doubt that cars provide fast, comfortable, and flexible personal transportation and have a valuable place in our transportation system, but their sheer popularity causes serious environmental problems. Changing from a car to a bike, even for just some of your journeys, will help improve the environment in which we live and work.

Our public spaces

If we could convert many unnecessary car trips to bicycle trips there would be a lot fewer cars on the streets, making more room for quality public space in our towns. Bicycles are not only the most energy-efficient transportation machine that humankind has invented, they are also among the most space-efficient.

In metropolitan areas space is at a premium, and a car-based transportation system needs a lot of space. The average car uses approximately four times the space of the average home: this includes parking spaces at the home, workplace, shopping center, supermarket, and town center; and these parking spaces are on average only occupied about 20% of the time!

Cars need a lot of road space. Road capacity is designed for rush hour, so although city streets may not be busy at midnight, during peak times congestion is a major problem, which is not only inefficient in time but also in fuel.

Bicycles take up less than 20% of the space of a moving car, and a comparatively tiny amount of parking space—a folding bike uses even less. If we convert just a few trips from car to bike, especially during rush hour, some of the space that was used for cars can be turned into quality public space for community recreation.

Air and noise pollution

Reducing the amount of cars in our cities will improve the air quality. Traffic noise causes stress, and in big cities there is almost no escape; but with fewer car trips and more bicycle trips we can have quieter, cleaner urban environments.

Safer communities

If each one of us gets on our bike we will reduce the number of cars on the roads, making a safer environment for the community and reducing the risk of accidents.

On average, 45,000 people die in car accidents in the United States every year.

Chapter 2

CAN YOU BIKE TO WORK?

To be honest, the sun is not always shining, big hills are difficult to climb, and not all offices have showers; but with the right route and the right equipment, these things are no big deal.

Planning the best route

Even if you live a long way from work it may still be possible to use your bike for all or part of the journey: you can take your bike on buses and trains, buy a folding bike, or leave your bike in a locker.

You will quickly discover that the routes you use by car are not usually the ones you would choose to use by bike. There are often great shortcuts that you can take on a bike, and sometimes the longer way can actually be better, for example, if there is a route beside a river, or through a park; your journey to work might take more time, but will become the highlight of the day.

First you'll need a good map. Check to see if your local municipality, local cycling groups, or bicycle shop have bike-specific maps with bike-friendly routes marked on them—they almost certainly do. Look on the Internet for maps and route advice for your area, and Google maps can be used to look at your route (see also chapter 7, page 63).

Start by getting a high-quality bicycle-route map— try asking your local city council, or download one from the Internet.

If you work for an organization that has a travel department, then you can ask for advice on the surrounding bicycle routes. Most human resources or facilities departments should also be able to help. There may also be a bicycle user group at work; they often meet once a month after work, and can help you find bicycle buddies to show you the best routes. Try to talk to anyone who bikes to work—tell them you are thinking about biking, and you'll find that they will be eager to share their secrets, just as you will be when you find that super shortcut through the park. If you can't find anyone to talk to, then it can be just as satisfying to be the pioneer.

Look at your current route, and if you are driving along a high-speed six-lane highway or really busy road, look to see if there are parks, smaller residential roads, or paths that you could use instead.

It is not a good idea to try a new route for the first time when you are rushing to get to work on time, so give it a try one weekend and look on it as good exercise. Once you have found

People often ask: What's in it for the bike rider? How much money does it save you to ride a bike? Do you know anyone who started doing this and got really fit?

The answers are that riding a bike to work is one of the most powerful daily actions that an individual American can make. It has powerful political implications, it is good for the environment, and it has vast benefits for public and personal health. But if people are not swayed by sentiment, then maybe the bottom line will be more convincing. In a city like New York, where everything has its cost, biking is the most economical way to get around.

— from Cycle NYC, courtesy of Transportation Alternatives (www.transalt.org)

a route you like, try to do it once without getting lost, and time yourself. Add about 10 minutes to allow for getting your bike out and locking it at your destination.

Integrating bikes with trains, buses, and cars

If you live too far from work to bike all the way, you can take a folding bicycle on a train and bike to and from the station. There may be other options: for example, a bicycle combined with a bus or train, or a friend's or colleague's car. If you are lucky, your home and your workplace will be close to stations on the same line—then you'll probably find a bicycle and train combination is the quickest way to commute.

Bicycles can be taken free of charge onto most trains; they usually fit in the space for wheelchairs (if not occupied). Some buses also

allow bikes, whether stored in the luggage compartment or carried on a bicycle rack on the front of the bus. However, not all trains have space for bikes, especially at rush hour. All is not lost, however, as a folding bicycle is always allowed, and if it is compact enough you can take it anywhere.

Folding bikes can also be fitted into the trunk of most cars. "Park and ride" takes on a whole new meaning with a bike in the trunk: parking on the edge of town and biking is usually the fastest and certainly cheapest way into the center, avoiding both traffic jams and excessive parking charges.

A good folding bike can be expensive, and is sometimes not as comfortable to ride as a full-sized bike; an alternative is to have two bikes. By riding one bike from your home to the station and keeping a second bike at the station close to your work, you can have all the convenience of a folding bicycle without the hassle of carrying it on the train.

Bicycles are solely human-powered and use no fossil fuels. Bicycles currently displace over 238 million gallons of gasoline per year by replacing car trips with bicycle trips. According to the Bureau of Transportation Statistics (BTS) October 2000 Omnibus Household Survey, 41.3 million Americans (20%) used a bicycle for transportation in the 30 days measured in the survey. Bicycling is the second-most-preferred form of transportation after the automobile, ahead of public transportation. More than 9.2 million (22.3%) of the 41.3 million people who bicycled did so more than ten of the 30 days measured. And, a short, four-mile round trip by bicycle keeps about 15 pounds of pollutants out of the air we breathe.

— courtesy of the League of American Bicyclists (www.bikeleague.org)

A two-bike combination is ideal where a bus trip makes up the bulk of the distance, and the bus does not allow for transport of your bike.

Looking good when you get there

Many people don't bike because they worry about looking like a sweaty beast or drenched rat if it rains on the way to work. Many workplaces now have showers; if yours doesn't, you could point out the advantages to your employer:

- the cost savings on parking spaces (which can cost thousands of dollars per year to maintain)
- the extra productivity of a healthy workforce
- the increased punctuality of cyclists compared to other commuters

They just might install one for you!

There are, however, some occasions when it is not easy, like going for an interview, or a meeting off-site where getting changed on arrival would be inappropriate. If you are not up for changing in restaurant restrooms, the solution is to either bike more slowly so you don't sweat, or to take the bus or car instead.

Many workplaces also have lockers where you can leave a clean set of clothes; it is quite easy to carry a towel, toiletries, and a change of clothes with you on a bike in panniers or a backpack. Breathable waterproof clothing will keep you dry when it is raining (see chapter 4, pages 33–40).

If you leave your work shoes at the office it saves a lot of weight in your bag; then all you need to carry is a change of clothes to start work looking smart and feeling fresh. Try to get to work 10 or 15 minutes early to give yourself a chance to cool down, tidy up, and change clothes.

Don't forget, however, that biking to work a few times a week will help you lose a few excess pounds, and although you don't have to look like Kate Moss to look good, you will feel better, and the change will probably be noticed by your loved ones. So maybe a few pounds off the beer belly might be worth a few hairs out of place once in a while.

Working up to the commute

How far is too far to cycle? It depends on how fit you are, how many hills there are, and how long you are prepared to take to get there. For a fit beginner forty minutes is about the limit: in forty minutes on relatively flat terrain a beginner cyclist should be able to cover up to eight miles at a comfortable pace.

Not all of us are 19 years old, super-fit with trim bodies to match, but if your office is less than five miles from your home, then no matter how old or unfit you may feel, why not give it a try.

Work up to it: practice on weekends, either on the route to work or just playing about with the family. Remember that cycling is not just for commuting. It is a sport and a leisure activity too, so a bit of practice will be fun—but the enjoyment is not always obvious if you are out of breath and sweating like a pig—just try to remember that it's good for you!

Finally, when you feel good about it, the weather looks good, and the evenings are long, go for it: try to bike all the way to work. See if you can convince one of your colleagues or neighbors whose workplace is near yours to join you in your quest, as a bit of company will make it much more enjoyable.

A great way to get to know other cyclists at your workplace is to organize a group ride during Bike-to-Work Week in May. Explore the local area for pleasant routes, and go on a group ride during the lunch break or after work. It's great fun, and a perfect way to find potential cycle buddies. Ideas and promotional materials are available from the League of American Bicyclists Web site.

Check whether your company is organizing a bikers' breakfast or rides for Bike-to-Work Week—a cook-out can be a welcome incentive.

Chapter 3

BUYING A BIKE

In the past twenty years bicycle design has undergone a revolution that has seen the introduction of bikes that can tackle all types of terrain, with space-age materials, multiple gears, suspension, and disc brakes. Walk into a bike shop these days and you are likely to see a vast array of bicycles with prices ranging from under $400 to well over $4000.

But even spending thousands of dollars won't guarantee you get the best bike for your needs; for instance, an expensive downhill bike with big wide knobby tires, disc brakes, and long-travel suspension might be perfect for riding over rough terrain down a mountainside but will be slow and heavy in the city.

Where to buy a bike

You don't need to go to a bicycle shop to buy a bicycle, as you can get them almost anywhere: online, in department stores, and by mail order. The advantage of buying your bike from a dedicated bicycle shop is that the sales staff are likely to be more knowledgeable and helpful in choosing the right bike for your needs.

The advantage of buying online from large retailers is that you can sometimes save money. The risk you take is that if you are unable to try the bike first, you will not be able to check that it is the right size. If you don't know much about bicycle design and components, the bike you buy might be cheap but not actually very good value. You generally get what you pay for, and if a bike looks too cheap to be true it probably is, as it is likely to be made with the cheapest parts and might be heavy and unreliable.

If you decide to buy through mail order or online, the bike is likely to be delivered only part-assembled and with untuned gears, brakes, and wheels. Although most quality online or mail-order companies will tune the bike before they box it, and all that is usually required is straightening the handlebars and putting on the front wheel and pedals (which is quite simple to do), it can seem difficult for the less mechanically proficient. A poorly assembled bike is dangerous to ride.

Finally, brake and gear cables will stretch after about 2 to 3 weeks of riding. A bike shop will usually give an after-sales service free of charge, and adjust the cables for you. If you buy online or at a department store you will need to do this yourself.

How much do bikes cost?

Bikes range hugely in price, but generally speaking a good new commuting bike will cost between $350 and $1,000. The price depends on the type of bike, the components that have been used to build it, the weight, and the brand. A more expensive bike will shift more smoothly through more gears, will be lighter, and possibly have a more comfortable saddle.

The bike you choose depends, among other things, on your budget, but for around $400 you can buy a pretty good bike to get around town, and an extra $100 will buy you all the extra parts and accessories you need to get started.

Maintaining and servicing the bike will probably cost around $60 a year, depending on how much you use it.

Over all, after calculating depreciation, maintenance, and the purchase of accessories, regular urban cycling can cost as little as $300 per year. The savings you make on city-center parking or

Since his election, Mayor Richard M. Daley has made it his goal to make the city of Chicago the most bicycle-friendly city in the United States. Mayor Daley has several bicycle ambassadors, with eight full-time staff, who teach drivers how to interact safely with cyclists, educate children on bike safety, and attend community events. The city recently completed a $3 million bicycle station in the central business district with indoor bike parking, showers, repairs, bike rentals, car-sharing services, guide bike tours, children's camps, and bike registration.

— courtesy of the League of American Bicyclists
(www.bikeleague.org)

public-transportation fares should cover this cost in a couple of months.

Secondhand bikes

If you work at a low-paying job and $400 would break the bank, then you can save money buying secondhand. Perfectly good bikes can be had for just a few bucks: try your local recycling center. Secondhand bikes are usually found in the local newspaper, on Web sites like eBay, from a market or yard sale, or sometimes reconditioned from your local bike store.

Your safest bet is to buy one that has been reconditioned from your local bike shop, as it will be tuned and ready to go. Buying secondhand from a bike shop also lessens the risk of getting a stolen bike—if the bike you purchase was stolen, you will lose it with no compensation.

When buying secondhand, check that the main components like gears and chain drive work well and smoothly, as these will cost the most to replace. Also check that the handlebars and pedals turn smoothly; if there is a grating sound, it is possible that the ball bearings have gone—replacing any of these is a difficult and expensive job.

Bikes that have been recovered by the police and remain unclaimed are often sold at auction. Check with local police departments to see if they hold a bike auction.

Size matters

There is a certain amount of personal preference in bike size, so there can be no better advice than to try the bike first before buying it. Nothing beats expert advice—talk to your local bike shop staff, and ask them to set the bike up for you.

As with shoes, getting the right size of bike will make a big difference to your comfort; but unlike shoes, there is a considerable amount of adjustment in the handlebar and saddle height of a bike, so it can be set up for you perfectly.

Bigger is not necessarily better An easy rule to follow when choosing your bike is that you should be able to reach the ground with your toes while sitting in the saddle. For bikes with a crossbar, when you are standing flat-footed there should be adequate clearance between the crossbar and your crotch; this is particularly important for guys in case you fall forward onto the bar while riding.

If you like to sit upright, go for the biggest frame that still allows crossbar clearance. If you prefer more athletic riding, particularly if you like to jump up and down from curbs and take the odd off-road route, you are safest with maximum clearance; so go for the smallest possible frame—as long as you can still stretch your legs and the bike isn't so short that it cramps your riding style.

On page 21 is a rough sizing chart of bike size in relation to inside leg —the distance from your crotch to the floor. The frame size is the length of the seat tube (the tube that the seat post and saddle are fixed into).

	INSIDE LEG		FRAME SIZE SUGGESTED	
	cm	in.	cm	in.
Mountain or hybrid bicycle	61–74	24–29	38	15
	64–76	25–30	41	16
	66–79	26–31	43	17
	69–81	27–32	46	18
	71–84	28–33	48	19
	74–86	29–34	51	20
	81–94	32–37	56	22
	INSIDE LEG		FRAME SIZE SUGGESTED	
Traditional, ladies, city bicycle	cm	in.	cm	in.
	64–76	25–30	43	17
	69–79	27–31	48	19
	74–84	29–33	53	21
	79–89	31–35	58	23
	INSIDE LEG		FRAME SIZE SUGGESTED	
Racing, touring bicycle	cm	in.	cm	in.
	71–81	28–32	50	19.5
	76–86	30–34	55	21.5
	81–91	32–36	58	23
	86–97	34–38	62	24.5

What type of bike do you need?

There are many different types of bicycle to choose from, each designed to perform a different function. Before buying a bike you need to consider what you will be using it for. If you want superfast commuting with the minimum of luggage, a road-race bike might be best; or if you are after a more comfortable bike, then a traditional city bike may fit the bill better.

Following is a list of the most suitable bikes for commuting, with general descriptions and the advantages and disadvantages of each. A lower, more aerodynamic posture will be faster as it cuts through the headwind, but may feel uncomfortable to riders who are not used to it; while upright postures are the reverse—very comfortable, but slower as it is harder to push against the wind.

Mountain bikes—all-terrain bikes (ATBs): $120–$6,000

Mountain bikes took the world by storm in the 1990s, and are still the best-selling design of bicycle. When the likes of Gary Fisher and Joe Breeze first started to launch themselves down the rocky slopes of the mountains of Marin County near San Francisco, few would have believed they were starting an industry. The converted old cruiser bikes they used in the 1970s have now morphed into myriad incarnations of mountain bike, each designed to cope with a slightly different terrain or riding discipline.

These days, although mountain bikes come in many shapes and sizes, the most suitable types for city riding are cross-country or all-terrain bikes (ATB). These both have tough frames, good brakes, lots of gears, knobby tires, suspension forks, and sometimes rear suspension. The cross-country bike design is to allow the rider to climb and descend off-road tracks at the fastest speed. The ATB is not as high performance as the cross-country bike, and is designed to withstand the rigors of rough treatment.

Both these designs are easy to control and will work well in the city, although it is recommended to swap the knobby tires for skinny ones, which are smooth-tread tires that offer lower rolling resistance on pavement.

Advantages Mountain bikes are strong, easy to control, and can be taken off-road on the weekends for a bit of fun. **Disadvantages** A good mountain bike has been designed for performance off-road, but it doesn't come with accessories to make city riding more comfortable, like mudguards or a wide saddle. It has a low posture, which may be uncomfortable, and off-road parts, like suspension, are expensive and unnecessary for urban cycling. Watch out for the cheap mountain bikes on the market—these can be very heavy, with poor-quality components, and would possibly break if actually taken off-road.

Road-racing bikes: $400–$12,000

Road-racing bikes are designed for speed. They are light, have larger diameter wheels with thin smooth tires for the minimum of rolling resistance, good brakes, many gears, and usually drop handlebars to make for a very low aerodynamic posture.

Some road bikes now have flat handlebars to give you a slightly more upright posture for added comfort and control—which can be useful in the city.

They usually have a higher gear range than a mountain bike, which makes them faster on the flat, but slightly harder to ride up very steep hills.

Some bicycle messengers in London choose to ride fixed-gear racing bikes. These have no gears, but when the wheel turns, so do the pedals, making for extremely efficient transmission and therefore high speeds on the flat, although steep hills can be a hard slog. These bikes are also more difficult to control.

Advantages Speed. There is no quicker way to ride around a city than on a road-racing bike. *Disadvantages* The price can be very high for a good road-racing bike, which can make them attractive to thieves. The thin wheels are not strong, making them prone to punctures and buckling if ridden over a big pothole.

Hybrid or trekking bikes: $300–$1,500

The hybrid or trekking bike is a mixture of the best elements of road and mountain bikes, and therefore very well suited to urban cyclists and leisure riders. They have larger diameter wheels, like road-racing bikes, but slightly wider rims and tires,

making them stronger. They maintain good speed on the road and give the rider good control and stability. Like mountain bikes, they come equipped with lots of gears and have good brakes.

Some versions come with suspension that is designed for a more comfortable ride rather than control when riding on difficult terrain. The better versions also come with wide, comfortable, sprung saddles, often made with high tech gel.

They have flat or riser handlebars that are curved upward to give an upright riding posture. Sometimes they also have an adjustable handlebar stem so the rider can adjust the handlebar height to attain the most comfortable posture.

A few hybrids come fully equipped with mudguards, rear luggage rack, and lights, which make them ideal for both leisure riding or regular commuting.

A new type of hybrid is the urban ATB, which, with smaller wheels, is closer to a mountain-bike design than a road-racing bike. They come with skinny tires for road riding, can be equipped with mudguards, and they have better handling but slightly less speed than an average hybrid.

Advantages When fully equipped, hybrids are perfect for commuting for the average rider. ***Disadvantages*** Not as fast as a road-racing bike or as tough as a mountain bike.

Traditional roadsters and city bikes: $340–$1,200

These are the classic designed bikes that everybody rode in the 1950s (and that people still ride in Holland and Denmark).

They are typically steel-framed and are either single speed or have internal hub gears with 3 to 7 speeds. They are fully equipped with mudguards, chain cover, lights, and rack, and sometimes even a dress guard. They have riser handlebars that are slightly angled upward, or have moustache handlebars that angle around like a moustache, giving a very upright riding position  that is often referred to as "sit-up-and-beg." They come in both a ladies' frame design (with a low step-through frame for easy access and riding in a skirt) and a traditional men's frame design with a high crossbar.

Advantages The upright posture makes them comfortable to ride and gives you good visibility. The chain cover, mudguards, and dress guard protect everyday clothing. The more modern bikes of this design often come from Germany or Holland and can be quite light. The easy-to-use hub gears are adequate for most cities and require much less maintenance than derailleur gears. *Disadvantages* They can be heavy and slower than other bike designs.

Folding and compact bikes: $300–$2,000

Folding bikes are perfect for commuters who come into the city by train, car, or bus, as they can be folded up and taken on public transportation.

The size of the wheels is anywhere from 12" to 26"—the smaller the wheels, the more compact the bike is when folded, but because of the size of the wheels they are less stable and the bike is not easy to ride fast. These bikes feel very nimble, but riding them can be  tiring if you spend long periods in the saddle.

There are many designs of folding bike, some easier to fold than others.

Advantages Small and compact, they easily fit on public transportation and have a small storage footprint. ***Disadvantages*** Less comfortable and slower to ride, they are also more expensive than a standard bike with the same parts specification.

Cruiser bikes: $360–$1,000

Cruisers were developed in the United States as big comfortable bikes with wide handlebars and big tires; they have a laid-back riding posture for cruising down the boardwalks and cycle paths, along beaches and through parks. They are generally brightly colored, with shiny mudguards and parts.

They were not designed for on-road riding, so their gears only have single, 3, 5, or 7 speeds, and they often do not have very good brakes—sometimes only a coaster brake on the back that works when you pedal backwards.

Recently they have been redesigned to be more suitable for road use.

Advantages They look stylish and feel comfortable over short distances. ***Disadvantages*** The wide handlebars are not good for heavy traffic, and they are often heavy and slow.

Comfort bikes: $500–$1,200

Like cruiser bikes, comfort bikes were also developed for leisure cycling. The comfort bike is a mountain bike that has a more upright cycling posture. It is designed for light off-road cycling along forest tracks and bicycle paths.

Comfort bikes are fitted with comfortable grips, smooth-rolling semi-thin tires, suspension on the front fork and seat post, as well as a comfortable saddle. Like mountain bikes, they come with many gears and good brakes.

Advantages They are very comfortable and easy to ride, and versatile enough to ride in the city and for leisure. *Disadvantages* They are slower than a hybrid bicycle, and never come fully equipped with mudguards or rear rack.

Electric bikes: $800–$3,000

Electric bikes supplement the rider's pedal power with a battery-powered motor. A torque sensor detects how hard the rider is pushing on the pedals and supplements this by battery power. Electric bikes can also come with a throttle like a motorbike, but all electric bikes are set to a maximum speed of 15 mph. They are very useful for hilly terrain, or for riders who do not want to strain themselves.

They come in all shapes and sizes, from electric mountain bikes to folding bikes. They have been on the market for over a decade, and although the original designs were heavy and unreliable, the technology has advanced in recent years and it is now possible to get a reliable, relatively low-cost bike with a fairly good range.

The key component is the battery; the best batteries are the lightest in weight and give the longest range.

- Lead acid batteries are the cheapest but also the heaviest, and will wear out the most quickly; they can be recharged up to 160 times.

- Nickel Metal Hydride (NiMH) batteries have good weight-to-power ratio and can be recharged up to 400 times.
- Lithium batteries are very lightweight and can usually be recharged over 1,000 times, but are very expensive.

Advantages Perfect for older or less able cyclists who want a little help, or for very hilly cities. ***Disadvantages*** They are heavier, more expensive, and cannot go any faster than 15 mph.

Bicycle components

Although the components such as the gears, brakes, rims, hubs, frame, and forks that are used to build your bike dictate the price, the relative advantages of all the various components could fill several books. Once you have decided what you need to use your bike for and how much you want to spend, if you get the right type of bike, then the right components will be mostly chosen for you. That said, there are one or two parts that you should consider carefully when choosing your bike.

Parts and accessories like mudguards, lights, and luggage carriers, although sometimes provided on a city bike, must often be bought separately (see chapter 4, page 39).

Saddles

Riding with the wrong saddle may make your experience of cycling decidedly uncomfortable, so choosing the right saddle is one of the most important decisions you make when buying a bike. There are as many designs of saddle as there are bikes, using a variety of advanced gels and shapes to avoid discomfort. It is not always the case that a softer saddle will necessarily be more comfortable; many traditionalists swear by the classic sprung leather saddle that molds itself to the shape of your posterior. Other cyclists prefer the cut-out designs that support the bones in your bottom but have a gap where pressure could cause discomfort.

Road-racing bikes have very thin saddles that regular road bikers think are comfortable, although the main reason for this design is to save weight.

City cyclists are likely to find a broader saddle more comfortable, and ideally you want to rest the center of your buttocks on the main part of the saddle. Bottoms come in all shapes and sizes, so before choosing a saddle for your bike it is recommended that you try it out first.

Suspension seat posts
Many comfort and hybrid bikes are now fitted with a suspension seat post, which is designed to absorb bumps from the road. They may make for a slightly more comfortable ride but are slightly heavier and can absorb energy from pedalling if not set up correctly.

Gears
The gears can be one of the most expensive parts of a bicycle, but, except in very hilly cities, you are unlikely to need many gears. There are two types of gear system available: derailleur and hub.

Derailleur A derailleur leads the chain from one sprocket to another while the chain is moving forward. There are usually two derailleurs on a bike: one on the front with 3 gears, and another on the rear with between 5 and 9 gears, offering a total of up to 27 possible combinations.

Advantages It is usually lighter than a hub gear, and therefore used on most high-performance bikes. With all the parts on the outside, if something goes wrong with a derailleur system it is easier to reach and fix; it is also slightly easier to take the back wheel off to fix a flat. **Disadvantages** A derailleur is a relatively high-maintenance system. As the chain is always shifting from one cog to another there is a lot of wear on the parts, and they are likely to need to be replaced

after a few years of use. You will need to oil the chain on a regular basis and adjust the gear cables to keep it from slipping. It is also possible that the chain may fall off while riding.

Hub gear Unlike the derailleur the hub gear has only one external cog, and the speed is controlled through cogs inside the hub of the rear wheel. There are many fewer speeds, usually between 3 and 7, but the ratio between the highest and lowest gear is usually similar to a derailleur system.

Advantages A hub gear is relatively low maintenance, although you should still oil the chain and may need to adjust the cable length—although this will be required much less often, and the hub system should last far longer. The chain is less likely to fall off from a hub gear system, and it is therefore recommended for city bikes. *Disadvantages* It is heavier, and if something does go wrong it is very hard to fix. It is also more difficult to remove the rear wheel.

Chapter 4

WHAT ELSE DO YOU NEED?

Once you have chosen the right bike there are still a few essential accessories you will need for cycling in a city, like a lock, some lights, and a pump. The right clothing, a few parts such as mudguards, and something in which to carry luggage will make your life more convenient and comfortable.

Clothing

You don't need any special clothing to ride a bike, and if you look at how the cyclists in places like Holland dress, you will see that they mostly wear everyday clothing; a skirt-guard, fully enclosed chain, sensible sit-up-and-beg-style bikes, and a vastly superior bicycle network make this possible. But if you plan to ride quickly through rush-hour traffic, or in the rain, then you should get some specialized cycling clothing to make you safer, more visible, and more comfortable.

Gloves Your hands need protection. They will feel very cold in the winter, and if you fall off your bike and you are not wearing gloves you will definitely hurt your hands. There are gloves on the market with all sorts of gels and padding to absorb road vibrations, but any set of gloves is better than none. Remember that you still need good grip and control when you buy your winter gloves.

Helmets There is some debate about the pros and cons of wearing a helmet (there is no legal requirement to do so in this country); but if you land on your head it could save you from brain damage. If you plan to go fast or tackle any off-road sections, you should definitely wear a helmet.

When buying a helmet make sure you get the right size, and fit it correctly. Buy the smallest helmet that is comfortable, to ensure it fits tightly on your head. Tighten the straps so that they feel tight when you have your mouth open. When trying your helmet on, remember that it is worn on top of the head, not tipped back.

Reflective vest To make sure that car drivers see you, wearing a reflective vest or reflective arm or leg bands makes sense when riding in a city. A few years ago a reflective vest would have seemed "uncool"; these days, at least in places where biking has become popular, they  could almost be considered a fashion accessory. You can get them from bicycle or hardware stores, and you can choose from a variety of different colors or designs, but with a can of spray paint, some scissors, cardboard, masking tape, and a bit of creativity, you can join the ubercool and customize your vest.

Specialized cycle clothing There is specialized clothing on the market that is designed to wick the sweat from your body to keep you cool in the summer and warm in the winter. Although not necessary for a leisurely commute, good-quality cycle clothing can make life much more comfortable on longer journeys. Mountain-biking gear has the same performance as tight-fitting road-biking gear, but is more baggy and may be more suited to those with less athletic bodies.

Shorts In the summer it is nice to change into shorts to ride, and cycle shorts come with a padded bottom that makes for a slightly more comfortable ride. You can buy baggy mountain-biking shorts if you are not a fan of Lycra.

Waterproof gear Cycle capes are the traditional way to ride in the rain and are great value, very efficient, and ideal if you get caught in the rain. They don't perform well in wind, however, so if you want to speed to work in all weather, breathable, lightweight waterproof jackets and pants are best. Priced from as little as $100, a good set will keep you pretty dry even in a major storm and can make riding in the rain seem almost fun. Traditional waterproof footwear or waterproof boots that fit over your shoes will keep your feet dry, although a couple of plastic bags held on by rubber bands will suffice in an emergency.

Keeping your head dry can be more difficult, and it is important not to obscure your visibility, so don't use a hood. You can get helmet covers or, if you prefer to ride without a helmet, a baseball hat with a peak; although not waterproof, this will keep the rain off your head and out of your eyes.

Chain guard Getting clothes caught in the chain can tear them or make them oily—a chain guard avoids this. Dutch bikes come with a completely enclosed chain, but the standard half guards that are fitted to many hybrid bikes are also good. Cycle clips are cheap and effective for keeping your pants away from the chain.

Lights

By law, if you ride in the dark you must have front, rear, wheel, and pedal reflectors, which should come standard on a new bike; in some places you also need a white front and a red rear light. Biking at night without lights is not only dangerous, it could cost you a fine in some cities. There are three main types of light:

Dynamo These are often prefitted on a fully equipped commuter's bike. They gain power from the turning wheels and do not require batteries. Prices vary, but a good set of dynamos will start at about $100. However, they go out when you stop and make the bike a bit harder to pedal.

LED (light-emitting diodes) Modern LEDs are very powerful, lightweight, and have a long battery life. Prices start at $12 for a set of two.

Halogen These give a strong beam of light so you can both see and be seen—particularly useful if you are riding on unlit roads. Their main disadvantage is the battery life; you will typically only get a couple hours use from alkaline batteries. You can get a rechargeable battery pack for around $80.

Locks and security

Having your bike stolen is pretty annoying, and protecting it from thieves is as much about choosing the right place to leave it as what lock you have. Compact folding bikes can be carried into the store, office, or home; the problem is that it is not always convenient or possible to carry one around all the time. Most workplaces and schools now have bicycle parking, which is also available in most city centers. A very public place will be the most secure. Having an old-looking bike (even if is actually valuable and new) is also a good bet, and you can cover your bike in electrical tape or paint, which will disguise the brand from a prospective thief.

No matter where you lock it, what lock you use, or how old and battered your bike looks, there is a chance that you will have your bike stolen. In order to trace it, It is worth recording the unique identity number that is stamped on every frame, usually on the underside of the bottom bracket. You should also record the model and make, and take a picture.

When locking your bike outside you should remember to also protect your wheels and seat post; quick-release bolts make adjusting the seat height or taking the wheels off very easy, but also offer easy pickings. If you sometimes leave your bike outside theaters and shops, it is probably worth swapping the quick-releases for conventional nuts and bolts. Otherwise, when you lock the bike be sure to lock the wheels to the frame and take the saddle with you.

A good bike lock is essential if you are going to leave your bike outside unattended; a modern-looking bike is more likely to be stolen than an old one. Thieves will take anything, so you should definitely buy a lock when you buy the bike, even if it is an old secondhand relic. Any lock can be broken by a professional thief, but as most bikes are stolen by opportunists using garage tools, the stronger the lock the less likely it is that your bike will be stolen.

There are hundreds of different locks on the market, ranging in price from $4 to $200, but as with most things, you get what you pay for. A good guide to what lock to buy can be found at the British Web site **www.soldsecure.com**.

Sold Secure "gold"-rated locks offer maximum security but are expensive and may be too bulky to carry easily, while "silver" and "bronze" levels should provide adequate protection. A simple way to decide what lock you need is to think where you will be leaving your bike, how long it will be unattended, and how much it is worth. Rather than carry a heavy expensive lock around with you, why not lock it where you park your bike (assuming you don't need it at the other end!)? All you need to carry then is your keys, which are much lighter.

Cable locks Coil and cable locks are easy to carry, can be looped around the bike, and are very flexible. Ideally you should choose a cable long enough to lock the wheels to the frame and to a cycle stand. Although very convenient, only very thick and strong cables are resistant to standard bolt cutters.

Chains Good thick chains and padlocks can be very heavy to carry, but the chain can be as long as you like. This is a good option if you lock your bike in high-risk areas for long periods.

U-Locks Heavy steel U-locks are strong and resistant to most bolt cutters, but can be harder to carry. They also do not have any flexibility, so it can be more difficult to find somewhere to lock the bike. Double-security locks provide both the security of a U-lock and have a long cable so you can still lock both wheels.

If you have an expensive bike and need to lock it outside, you can disguise it to deter thieves. Try wrapping the frame in tape or use paint to make it look old and ugly.

Luggage carriers

Carrying luggage on a bike is simple, whether it is your laptop, paperwork, or dress clothes.

Backpacks Backpacks will make your back sweat, so are not ideal when you are wearing your work clothes. However, they can be fitted with a laptop insert and are good for carrying both your laptop and work clothes if you don't have panniers.

Briefcase pannier This is designed to fit onto the luggage rack, and looks sharp and professional when carried by hand; a briefcase pannier fits a standard laptop, and usually has room for clean clothes and some papers.

Basket and handlebar bags These hook onto the handlebar and are a convenient way to carry small loads. Classic ladies' bikes are usually fitted with a basket, and are very convenient for holding a few items if you are using your bike around town. Wicker or metal are both available, as well as bags made of other materials.

Standard panniers One single-side pannier offers plenty of space to cram in most things you could want at work, and you can get fully waterproof designs, pannier covers, or waterproof inserts to keep your clothes dry if it rains.

Wedge bags that fit under the seat are a great way to carry the essential tools for emergency repairs.

Trailers Trailers are the best way to carry really large or heavy loads. The main disadvantage is that a trailer increases the length of the bike, making it more difficult to control and ride in a city.

Rear luggage rack If you want to carry panniers, then you will need a luggage rack: you should choose one that has two or three legs that provide wide side support for the load. Welded luggage racks are the strongest, followed by bolted racks; the type that clamps onto the seat post is the weakest. Once you have a rack you should also buy some bungee cords or cargo net to hold down the odd load like rain gear (or your jacket if it gets too hot).

Mudguards

Without mudguards, the spray from your wheels on a wet road will splash all over you. Modern mudguards are made of advanced plastics that are light and almost unbreakable. Prices start at around $40 for a set.

There are two types: full-wheel and quick-fix. Full-wheel are recommended if they fit your bike, as they catch all the road spray, while quick-fix are suitable for mountain bikes that often cannot take standard mudguards.

Tools

A pump, a multitool, and a tire-repair kit can all be carried with you—see chapter 6, pages 51–52 for more information.

Chapter 5

GETTING STARTED

As the old phrase goes, "It's like riding a bike": once you learn you never forget. Most of us had bikes as children and can still ride one. Is there anything that adults need to learn about riding a bike?

There are more cars on the road than ever before, and surveys show that the biggest barrier to taking up riding a bicycle is the perception of danger. Confident cyclists who have good road position and excellent control of their bikes are the safest. If it has been several years since you were last on a bike, and the prospect of riding on a busy road is daunting, then a few hours of training with experienced riders will do wonders for your confidence and safety.

Before you ride on the road

Before jumping on the bike and launching yourself onto the open road, here are a few tips:

Have a roadworthy bike A bike bought from a bike shop should be ready to ride. If you already have a bike, seek the advice of a mechanic at a bicycle shop or use the checklist below:

- **Brakes** Look to see if the brake pads look worn. Lift the front wheel, spin it, and pull the front brake: the wheel should immediately stop turning. Repeat with the rear wheel.
- **Tires** Test with your thumb to see that the tires are firm, if not, pump them up.
- **Wheels** Check that the wheels are true: lift the front wheel and spin it to make sure it is not impeded, and repeat with the rear wheel. Check that the wheels are clamped securely.

- **Handlebars** Hold the front wheel between your legs and wiggle the handlebars to ensure they are tight and aligned correctly.
- **Saddle height** You should be able to sit in the saddle and touch the ground with your toes.
- **Test ride** Before venturing onto a road, the final check should be a test ride. Find a safe, car-free area and take a ride, operating the brakes and gears, and making sure the bike is comfortable. Do not ignore strange noises or jumping gears, as they probably indicate a problem.

Bicycle maintenance is covered in chapter 6, but if you have any doubts about the mechanical safety of your bicycle, seek help from your local bike shop.

If you have never ridden a bike before, consider starting with a ladies' bike with a low, step-through frame. Stand with legs astride the bike, hold the handlebars, put one foot on a pedal, push forward with the other foot and start pedaling. You may wobble a bit at first, but the faster you go the less you will wobble.

Steering To get used to steering your bike, try practicing maneuvering between some obstacles, and making U-turns.

Signaling and communication Probably the most important part of riding on the road is good communication with other road users. Before you take to the road you should practice riding with one hand, and looking behind while signaling. Before you maneuver, make sure there are no obstacles in front, and then look behind you and try to make eye contact with approaching drivers. Always clearly signal what you are going to do.

Braking There are two brakes on a bike, front and back; the back brake is usually operated by the left hand and the front brake by the right hand. Both levers are on the handlebars. These are the most important part of the bike, so get used to the brake setup and to operating it.

Practice in a car-free area, and get used to riding with your fingers on the brake levers. If this is very uncomfortable, or if you find the brakes are not working well, seek the advice of a mechanic at a bike shop.

Use the back brake to slow down, and both front and back brakes together to stop.

Emergency stops To stop quickly, simultaneously pull hard on the back and front brakes, shift your weight backwards, moving your posterior toward the back of the saddle while stiffening your arms. It sounds more difficult than it is; practice a few times.

- **Avoid skidding** Pulling the back brake hard will lock the rear wheel, which will cause you to skid. Like ABS in cars, brakes work most effectively when the wheels are still turning. If you start to skid, release the brake lever slightly.
- **Do not pull the front brake on its own suddenly** as this could throw you over the handlebars. When using the front brake, shift your weight toward the back of the bike.
- **Never turn the handlebar while pulling hard on the front brake**—the front wheel will skid, and you could lose control.

Operating the gears Many bikes have gears, which make it both easier to climb hills and get high speeds on the flat. Unless you live in a very hilly area you are unlikely to need more than a few gears for everyday use. Most gears are controlled from the handlebar either as grip shifters or as EZ-fire (buttons that are pressed by thumb and forefinger), or incorporated into the brake levers.

There are two main types of gears—derailleur and hub—which are operated differently. Each has advantages and disadvantages (see chapter 3, pages 30–31).

With **derailleur** gears, you change gear while pedaling forward. The front derailleur is controlled from the left-side shifter, the rear derailleur from the right shifter. Different gear speeds are achieved from combinations of the front and rear derailleurs.

On the front, the largest sprocket is the highest gear, while on the back the smallest is the highest gear. A 27-speed bike will have 3 speeds on the front and 9 on the rear, giving 27 possible combinations. However, try to avoid the gears that make the chain cross over at an extreme angle; these "criss-cross" gears are bad for the chain and sprockets. Especially bad is to combine the inside (small) front sprocket with the outside (small) rear sprocket; this combination is noisy, inefficient, and causes the chain to wear out prematurely.

With **hub** gears you briefly stop pedaling to change gear. A hub gear only has one external cog, and the speed is controlled through cogs inside the hub of the wheel. There are fewer gears, usually between 3 and 7, but this system is easier to operate and the ratio between the highest and lowest gear is usually the same as a 27-speed derailleur system.

Be visible

Before you enter traffic you should ensure that you are visible: wear a reflective jacket or vest and have lights on your bike if you might be cycling in the dark.

On the road

Once you have learned to control your bike, and are confident with turning, braking, and changing gears, you are ready to ride on the road, but before you do you should be aware of the basics of road position.

There are two main positions for on-road cycling. You can ride in the traffic stream (the primary position) or to the right of it (the secondary position).

Primary position If riding in the middle of a lane you are part of the traffic, and are very visible to drivers because you are right in front of them. This position should be adopted in residential streets, especially when parked cars on either side may mean there is not enough room for safe passing. You are also doing drivers a favor by removing the decision from them as to whether or not there is room to squeeze past you.

Secondary position Riding to the right of the traffic stream, in the secondary position, is a concession to road users coming from behind at higher speeds, allowing them to pass. This position is usually adopted on main roads.

The distance from the curb depends on the width of the road, but as a rule of thumb leave at least three feet between yourself and the curb.

Inexperienced cyclists often ride too close to the curb. This is dangerous, because if you hit a bump, or a car door opens, or a pedestrian or pet runs out in front of you, you can only swerve into the traffic stream. But if you are further away from the curb and someone passing gets too close, you still have room to move back toward the right. Generally, cars will give you as much room as you give yourself.

Passing parked cars When passing parked cars, always be aware that a car door could open, so look to see if the cars are occupied.

Taking the lane There are occasions where you should move from the secondary to the primary position. This is called "taking the lane."

Places where you should take the lane include:

- passing parked cars
- approaching and moving through an intersection

- riding in a bus lane
- moving through a narrowing road

—in fact whenever you want to ensure you are not going to be passed. To do so, plan well ahead, and look over your left shoulder to see if it is clear. If it is clear far enough behind so that no one will be affected, move left into the traffic stream. You may have to wait. Good communication and signaling should enable you to negotiate your way into the traffic stream.

Intersections Approaching traffic lights or an intersection where you must give way, position yourself in the primary position in the center of the lane. If when approaching an intersection there is a line of traffic, the least safe option is to pass on the right, so be very cautious and never pass a truck or large vehicle on the right. It is best to either wait your turn or consider passing on the left to get to the front, where there is often a reserved area for cyclists.

Clearly signal your right or left turn, and look behind to check that drivers are giving way. Then when it is clear, or the lights are green, move through the intersection maintaining your primary position in the center of the lane.

Rotaries Rotaries are the most dangerous places for inexperienced cyclists. To be safe, it is very important to signal clearly and maintain communication with other road users. At a rotary, because visibility is all-important, you should arrive at, and move through, in the middle of the most appropriate lane. Look all around you and signal your intentions clearly.

Chapter 6

BICYCLE MAINTENANCE FOR BEGINNERS

Keeping your bike on the road

Part of the beauty of bicycle design is its simplicity, which means that the common repair jobs are not difficult to do yourself. If you have an absolute aversion to getting your hands dirty, however, in most towns and cities there are plenty of bicycle shops where a mechanic will happily fix anything from a puncture to a bottom bracket at relatively low cost. Be aware that expensive performance bikes are likely to require more maintenance than city bikes.

Most bike shops also provide servicing, and since keeping your bike well maintained will ensure it works better and lasts longer, taking it for a regular service will probably save you money. If you completely disregard bicycle maintenance you are more likely to encounter mechanical problems that will be difficult and expensive to fix.

Only the very basics of bicycle maintenance are covered here, but if you aspire to be a trained mechanic, there are courses you can take and plenty of further reading you can do.

The essential tools

The following tools are recommended for basic bicycle maintenance.

- *Cycle oil* You must keep your chain well oiled, and for the minimum trouble, traditional cycle oil, also known as wet lube, is ideal. It will stay on your chain even in the rain and keep your chain lubricated for a relatively long time. Dry lube, often with an additive like PTFE or Teflon, will lubricate your chain and has the advantage of keeping it clean, preventing the buildup of dirt. It washes off in the rain, however, so you will need to regularly reapply it.

- **Latex gloves and a rag** Bicycles get dirty, and you will need an old rag to wipe off excess oil. As you probably don't want to get filthy hands, a pair of latex gloves, although not essential, are a very useful part of a tool kit.

- **Multitool** Individual tools will be easier to use, but a multitool comes in an easy-to-carry package and has most of the tools you need for basic bicycle maintenance. There are many versions on the market, but ideally a multitool should have at least an Allen wrench set, flat and Phillips screwdrivers, and a set of spanners.

- **Pump** Tires lose pressure over time, and when they do they have greater rolling resistance. Pumping up your tires is quicker and easier with a big chamber floor pump that you can keep at home, and a mini-pump that is easily carried on the bike.

- **Tire repair kit** A tire repair kit should include tire levers, patches, and rubber cement. New self-adhesive patches are now also available, and are easier to use, but more expensive.

The absolute basics

Even if you suffer from chronic mechanical incompetence and were almost entering high school before you learned to tie your shoe laces, there are a couple of very easy jobs that you should be able to do yourself to keep your bike in good working order.

Lubricating your chain If you start to hear squeaky noises from your chain when you ride, then it needs lubrication; if you continue to ride with a dry chain, more expensive parts will wear out very quickly. To lube the chain, simply apply chain oil to the entire length of the chain as you turn the pedal backwards, being careful not to allow oil to leak onto the rim of the rear wheel, which will affect your braking. It is best to clean your chain before oiling: special degreasers can be bought from a bike shop.

Pumping up the tires You will need to pump them up a little bit about once a month. There are two common bicycle tube valves: Presta and Schrader—check which type your bike has. Most pumps can be set to inflate either valve type, so simply adjust your pump to the correct valve setting and inflate the tires until they feel solid when pressed with your thumb. It is possible to overinflate with a floor pump, so stop pumping when the tire feels hard. If your pump has a pressure gauge, inflate to the recommended pressures stamped on the sidewall of the tire.

Presta valve *Schrader valve*

Common repairs

Flat tires

There is no more annoying or common problem than a flat tire, so the best advice is to be careful where you ride: it goes without saying that you should avoid glass on the road and other tire hazards.

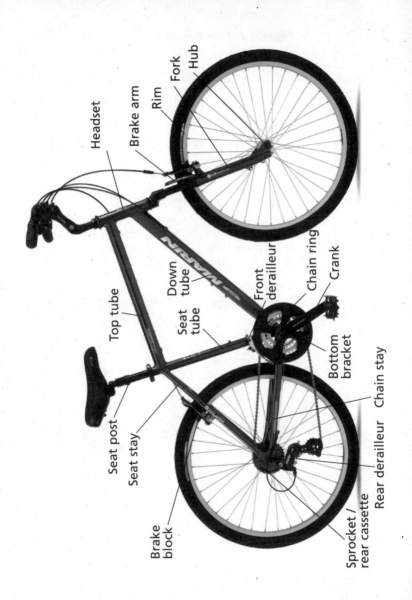

Buy a bike fitted with puncture-resistant tires or fit them yourself. There are many types available. You can also buy a puncture-resistant strip and line your tires yourself. There are inner tubes available that are filled with puncture-resistant goo—the best known is "Slime," which reacts with air to automatically seal a puncture if you get one. No prevention system is foolproof, and when you hear the inevitable hiss of escaping air you should stop riding and either repair it yourself or push it to the nearest bike shop.

Fixing flats If you have quick-release wheels, it is usually easier to remove the wheel to work on a flat, although it should be possible to fix the tire while the wheel is still on.

1. Release the brakes You will need to release your brakes to get access to the tube or to remove the wheel.

V-brakes: Press the top of the two brake arms together and disengage the cable to allow the arms to spring apart.

Other brakes: Road bikes and some folding bikes have side-pull brakes. These often have a switch that releases the brake blocks from the wheel, or you may have to remove one of the brake blocks with an Allen key. When you buy a bike, ask for instructions on how to release the brakes so that you can remove the wheel.

2. Remove the wheel After releasing the brakes you can remove the wheel. If you have quick-release skewers, you simply open the quick-release lever and take the wheel off, twisting the nut slightly to open it wider if the wheel will not come off easily. If removing the rear wheel you will need to take it off the chain, which will be much easier if the chain is on the smallest outside cog in top gear.

If you do not have quick-release wheels you will need the right-sized spanner to loosen the axle nuts, but otherwise the process is the same.

If you have hub gears, you will need to unscrew the cable brake in order to remove the wheel.

3. Check the tire visually to see if you can spot where the tire has been punctured; run your hand along the tire to feel for a sharp object, which if found should be removed. Make a mental note of the position of the puncture on the wheel if you can find it.

4. Remove the tube Ideally take three tire levers, wedge them under the tire and pull it up and over the wheel rim, using the spokes to fix them in place. Be careful not to catch the inner tube with the lever, or you might cause another puncture.

Take another tire lever and use it to lever the tire off the rim, an inch or so along from the first lever, to widen the gap. Continue to widen the gap in this way using the third lever, until it is possible to run a lever around the rim to fully remove one side of the tire.

Remove the valve cap and threaded metal collar if there is one, and empty the tube of any remaining air. Push the valve back through the hole in the rim, and carefully pull the tube out from under the tire.

5. Find the hole Once out, inflate the inner tube and listen or feel for the escaping air; if you have water handy, you can submerge the tube in water and watch for bubbles.

6. Apply a patch With a traditional tire repair kit, clean the area around the hole, then dry it, put a dab of rubber cement on the hole, and using your finger, gently spread it in a small circular area around the hole. Wait for the solution to dry, apply the patch, and push hard to make sure there are no air bubbles. When you are happy the patch is secure, you can grate some chalk on the area to prevent the inner tube sticking to the tire when it is replaced. If you have self-adhesive patches, you only need to find the puncture and clean and sand the tube before applying the patch.

7. Check for more holes Reinflate the inner tube and check its entire length for more holes.

8. Check for sharp objects Before you put the tube back, you must ensure the sharp object that caused the puncture has been removed. Use a finger to feel along the whole of the inside of the tire, checking the area where the inner tube was punctured particularly carefully.

9. Replace the tube Remove all air from the tube, place the valve back into the rim, and work the tube back under the tire onto the wheel. Hook the tire back onto the rim with your hands; you may need to use a tire lever to hook the last section back onto the tire. Be very careful not to pinch the tube between the tire and rim, as this could cause another puncture. Replace the threaded collar and pump up the tire.

Cables

Cables are used on bicycles for operating the brakes and gears. Cables stretch and sometimes snap, and occasionally need tightening and replacing. Cable stretch is particularly pronounced when the cables are new; because of this, most bicycle shops will give a free tune-up a few weeks after you buy a new bike.

Tightening your brake cable If you can pull the brake lever until it almost touches the handlebar grip, then you need to tighten the cable.

Small adjustments can be made with threaded adjusters, which are usually found either where the cable comes out of the brake lever, or sometimes where the cable goes into the brakes. Simply unscrew this to extend the cable until your brakes feel tighter. After making an adjustment, twist the threaded outer locking nut back to the brake lever to lock the new position in place.

For bigger adjustments, follow the cable down from the brake lever to the other end, where you will see it is locked in place with a clamp bolt. Loosen this nut, using an Allen key or nut wrench, to allow the cable to move freely. Pull the cable through with your fingers or pliers until the brake blocks are positioned just a couple of millimeters on either side of the rim; then securely tighten the clamp bolt.

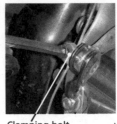

Clamping bolt

After adjusting the brakes, always check that the wheel turns freely and that the brakes work well before riding again.

Tightening your gear cable Derailleur gear cables occasionally stretch, which will make your shifting inaccurate. Small adjustments can be made with twist adjusters where the cable comes out of the shifter on the handlebars. Simply turn the adjuster one or two revolutions to tighten the cable slightly, and continue to turn until the gears are back in sync.

To make further adjustments, turn the bike upside down and you will see another adjuster where the cable goes into the gears by the rear wheel. Turn this adjuster a revolution or two. To check if the gears are in sync, simply turn the pedals while the bike is upturned and shift through the gears.

Adjuster   Clamping bolt

For bigger adjustments, put the bike into high gear, loosen the clamping bolt, and pull the cable through while pushing the derailleur in slightly with your hand. Tighten the clamping bolt and check again to see if the gears are in sync.

Replacing a brake cable Cables not only stretch—they can also snap if not maintained properly. This happens most often with brake cables; if it does, you should stop riding immediately. You will also need to replace the cable if the cable housing becomes frayed or bent, as it will make the cable stick. Regularly check for frayed cables and cable housing.

To replace a cable you will also need cable cutters or a hacksaw, and tiny cable caps to put on the end of the cable to prevent it from fraying.

1. Undo the cable at the far end by loosening the clamping bolt.

2. As you remove the old cable, place the parts in a line so that you can easily see where everything goes. Even if you're planning to replace the housing, keep the old sections so you can cut the new pieces to match.

3. With the cable loose, pull the lever all the way back to the handlebar; this will expose a hole that contains a knob on the end of the cable. Line this knob up with the hole and push it out.

4. When released, pull the cable out from the brake-lever end.

5. If replacing the cable housing, get the cable cutters or a hacksaw to cut the pieces the same size as those you have removed.

6. Insert the new cable through the brake lever, ensuring that the round knob at the cable end is fitted securely back into the hole. Then begin assembling the sections of cable housing onto the cable. If you are replacing cable housing you will need to fit a metal cap or cable stop onto every end. Fit the housing into the mountings at the brake lever, and at each mounting of the frame.

7. Pull the cable back through to the clamping bolt, adjust the brakes to the correct position, and tighten the clamping bolt to secure. Check that the brakes now work properly and adjust the position if necessary.

8. Use the cable cutters to cut off excess cable, take a cable cap and place it on the end of the cable, and use pliers to compress the cable cap so it stays on the end.

Replacing brake pads

With regular use, brake pads (or blocks) will require replacing. If the brakes are tight but still do not work very well, then you probably need to replace the brake pads; never allow them to wear through to the metal, as this will quickly destroy your wheel rims, which are expensive to replace, while a set of brake pads can be bought for just a few dollars.

When replacing with the new pads, be sure that they are aligned properly with the wheel rim. After they are tightened, pull the brake to check that they do not rub against the tire, as this will cause a puncture.

Cleaning your bike

To keep your bike in good working order and to prolong its life, give it a good cleaning once in a while. There are several cleaning fluids on the market that when diluted and sprayed on the bike will cut through the dirt and oil to make this job easier. After cleaning, do not forget to re-oil the chain. There are many eco-friendly bike cleaners on the market.

More difficult repairs

Replacing gear cables, adjusting your gears, straightening buckled wheels, or replacing a spoke are all repair jobs that you can also learn to do yourself and are worthwhile if you plan to take your bike on a long adventure; however, they require a degree of skill. For the beginner it is much easier to take your bike to the local bike shop and have it repaired by a professional.

Several cycling and sustainable transport Web sites give information about maintenance: see pages 81–83.

Chapter 7

IS YOUR WORKPLACE BICYCLE-FRIENDLY?

Ten years ago it was hard to find even a single bicycle parking stand at an office. Nowadays, realizing that an urban parking space can cost thousands of dollars a year to maintain, many workplaces have installed secure bicycle shelters. Some have state-of-the-art changing rooms, and a few even provide cash incentives to encourage their staff to bike to work instead of driving, as part of their organization's travel plan. Travel plans were first developed as part of the solution for the air-pollution problems in California. A travel plan is a package of measures to promote car sharing, car clubs, public-transportation use, and walking and biking.

Even though great progress has been made toward making more places bicycle-friendly, many workplaces still have no facilities for cyclists. Even where organizations are working to promote biking, their effectiveness depends on the participation of everyone.

Bicycle parking

Having a secure place to leave your bicycle is essential, although it is often possible to lock bicycles to railings, lampposts, or parking meters. However, this looks untidy, is in full view of potential thieves, provides no protection from the elements—and the popular places are often full. Organizations that provide good-quality bicycle parking send a message to staff and visitors that cycling is valued.

In 2005, Davis, California, received the Platinum award from the League of American Bicyclists for its efforts to create a bike-friendly community. According to the League, there are more bikes in Davis than there are cars, and at the time it was the only community that had two full-time bike coordinators, plus staff, and two bicycle advisory committees. Bike lanes can be found on roughly 95% of the city's main arterial and collector roads, and the city has 27 different grade separations for bicycles and pedestrians. The city recently spent $7.4 million to build a bicycle underpass of a two-lane country road, six lanes of Interstate 80, and two sets of railroad tracks. To top it off, the city's logo is a bicycle, and nearly 20% of work commutes are made by bicycle. Years ago, this city of 65,000 people voted to get rid of all public school buses, so many children walk or bike to school.

— courtesy of the League of American Bicyclists (www.bikeleague.org)

There is a wide variety of bicycle parks available, from a simple covered bicycle shed to impressive futuristic designs. For small offices or apartments, however, a simple hook or wall attachment can be fitted very inexpensively. Where possible, cycle parking should be placed in a secure location to discourage thieves, either in clear view of the office, or as part of an underground parking garage if there is one.

It is just as important to have somewhere safe to park your bike at home. If you lack space, then there are bicycle storage-solutions that hang from a wall, but if you live in an apartment or multistory house with no room to store a bicycle inside, a wall hook and a strong lock should keep the bicycle secure outside.

Showers and changing rooms

It is nice to be able to change and shower before you start work. Providing high-quality facilities for cyclists is a clear signal that the employer values staff who choose to bike instead of drive, and when car parking costs so much to maintain, it makes good business sense.

Consequently many large employers have fitted extensive changing rooms for cyclists, close to bicycle parking. These include lockers, showers, and even ironing boards. Employers should take care when allocating lockers that there is a system in place to ensure they are in regular use. There have been cases when lockers are still allocated to staff who don't ride regularly or who have even left the company.

For small businesses without the budget for such extensive facilities, just the addition of a shower in the restroom is sufficient to cater to the needs of an employee who wishes to bike to work.

Bicycle-user groups (BUGs)

In many large organizations bicycle-user groups are formed to discuss anything from bicycle maintenance to the best routes to and from the office. They are also excellent ways to meet fellow cyclists who may bike in a similar direction and might be interested in becoming bicycle buddies, biking to and from work together. Ask in the office if there is an existing BUG; if not, you can form one with just a few posters or an e-mail to everyone in the company.

Incentives to ride

As mentioned in chapter 1, a healthy workforce is more productive and absent fewer days, and regular cycling is one of the best ways to get and stay healthy. Cyclists are statistically the

Though Davis, California, has the most bikes per capita, Portland, Oregon (population 533,000), is considered perhaps the most bike-friendly city for a large urban area. Almost every action taken by the city—from the mayor to street crews—seeks to promote increased use of bicycles. The city has a growing network of bike lanes (nearly 170 miles), and trails (nearly 70 miles). In 1992, there were 3,555 daily bike trips across the city's main bridges, and that increased to 8,250 by 2002, and then nearly doubled again to 14,563 in 2006.

This rapid increase has been helped by some recent improvements to its overall network of lanes, trails, and signed routes:

- *Bicycle-only signal heads at two key city intersections*

- *Shared-lane pavement markings*

- *700 bicycle-boulevard pavement markings along 30 miles of streets*

- *350 distance and destination signs at bikeway intersections that show riding times to major destinations*

- *Bicycle-only scramble signal at a critical trail/roadway intersection*

- *Colored bike lane markings at specific conflict areas*

Then, there is Portland's Bike Central, which provides bicycle commuters with clothes storage, showers, and secure bike parking. The city has also eliminated the need for permits to put bikes on the city's buses and light rail cars, and eliminated the peak-hour, peak-destination restrictions on carrying bikes on public transit.

— courtesy of the League of American Bicyclists (www.bikeleague.org)

The potential to increase the numbers of people bicycling to work in the United States in the very near future is even more impressive. San Francisco and other cities more than doubled bicycle commuting between 1990 and 2000 through investment in bike lanes, trails, bike parking, maps, education programs, encouragement activities, and a focused bicycle plan; however, there is much more we can do. The 2000 Census reported that there are 500,000 bicycle commuters in the United States—less than half of one percent of journeys to work and woefully short of the percentages in Canada (1.2%), the United Kingdom (2%), Germany (11%), Denmark (20%), and the Netherlands (27%).

Bicycling to work, moreover, is just part of the picture. We know that more than three quarters of trips made today aren't for commuting. They are social or recreational, for shopping or the like. Amazingly, the 2001 U.S. National Household Travel Survey (NHTS) tells us that in our metropolitan areas more than 40% of those trips are two miles or less—a very manageable bike ride—and more than one-quarter are just one mile or less.

Survey after survey shows that people want to ride and walk more but are dissuaded by concern over traffic danger and other barriers. When barriers to bicycling are removed, people start riding. As a case in point, Portland, Oregon, has seen bicycle use quadruple since 1994 as their bike network has grown from 60 miles to 260 miles. They have also invested in cyclist and motorist education, encouragement programs, simple measures such as providing bike parking, and fully integrating transit, walking, and bicycling.

— Andy Clarke, executive director, League of American Bicyclists, in Congressional testimony delivered on May 16, 2007 most punctual employees, and a bicycle takes up a lot less parking space, saving employers money. These advantages have led some employers to even offer their staff incentives to get out of the car and onto a bicycle.

Incentives vary from a "bike miles" token card, which is stamped every time the employee arrives by bicycle and when full can be redeemed against free cycling gear, to a free biker's breakfast once a month.

Salary-sacrifice plans

The British government started a plan a few years ago whereby employees can buy a bike through their employer at up to 50% discount off the retail price. The money is taken directly from the employee's gross salary, saving on Income tax.

There are companies that will help an employer set up a salary-sacrifice plan, which can even be implemented at very small companies. Check with your HR department to see if your company has such a plan.

Company bikes

Many workplaces are in industrial parks that are a few miles from the center of town, which means employees drive to work so they have access to a car for lunch breaks or local meetings. Some organizations therefore provide a few company bikes, which any member of staff can borrow for a few hours to go to a local meeting or to get something for lunch.

City-based organizations find that the provision of a few company bikes can significantly reduce taxi use and save the company money.

Bike servicing

The provision of once-monthly on-site bike servicing by a bike mechanic from a local bicycle store is also a great way to

Bike commuting in New York is easy and makes sense. In fact, 25% of car trips in the city are less than one mile, while 72% are less than five miles, meaning that the average commute by bike would take 30 minutes. This nicely trumps the average commute for all city residents, which is 45 minutes (the longest average commute in the United States). After all of the time and frustration a person saves by getting to work on their bike, there is still even more good news: A roundtrip, 30-minute bike commute will burn, on average, 440 calories.

— from Cycle NYC, courtesy of Transportation Alternatives (www.transalt.org)

encourage staff to ride, and is important if the company has pool bikes.

Bike-to-Work Week

In the third week of May every year, the League of American Bicyclists promotes Bike-to-Work Week, a nationally coordinated week of bicycling events. It is an opportunity for employers to get as many staff as possible to try cycling. In 2007, thirty-four states and the District of Columbia held special biking events in big cities and small towns, including group rides and tours, free bike tune-ups, free coffee and breakfast, free concerts and T-shirts, raffles, giveaways, speeches, dinners, and farmer's markets. Anyone can organize a Bike-to-Work Week event. Check out the League of American Bicyclists Web site at www.bikeleague.org.

Bicycle training

Employers that wish to encourage their staff to cycle often organize free bicycle training to encourage less confident cyclists to give it a try.

Chapter 8

IT'S NOT ALL WORK

Cycling is not just a great way to get to work—it is also a great way to spend your free time. Whether it is taking the family on a ride along a bicycle path, joining a bike club to ride at speed on a road bike, performing death-defying stunts on a BMX, crossing the Alps on a bike adventure, or charging down a gnarly trail on a mountain bike, cycling can be a lot of fun. All of us can remember the excitement of riding a bike as a child, and if it's been a while since you were last on a bike, you'll probably be surprised that it can be just as exciting as an adult.

Leisure cycling

The popularity of cycling as a way to get around has grown in recent years, as have the opportunities for leisure cycling. Cities and towns across the United States have responded to this trend by allocating budget dollars for networks of bike paths, greenbelts, and multiple-use recreation trails connecting urban and suburban areas. Many sections of these networks are car-free and pass through scenic landscapes, whether on old railroad beds or along waterways and waterfronts. Contact your local city hall for more information about bike paths, maps, and cycling opportunities in your area.

A National Bicycle Route Network is being developed by the Adventure Cycling Association in tandem with the American Association of State Highway Transportation Officials and other organizations. Though still in the planning stages, the goal is to create a "national interstate route system" of scenic roads and trails stretching from coast to coast. Find out more about the NBRN and designing your own bike tour at www.adventure cycling.org.

The car-free sections of an urban or suburban bike network are perfect for a family day out with the kids, the grandparents, or with a boy- or girlfriend, stopping by a restaurant en route for a drink and a meal.

There are many leisure bicycling events organized across the country, and you can find them by using the Internet or by inquiring at your local bike shop.

Many of the events are also run for the benefit of charities such as cancer research, so if you do take part, you could look into raising sponsorship money for a good cause.

Mountain biking

When the first mountain bikers hurled themselves down the mountains in California on converted cruiser bikes, few would have believed they were launching an Olympic sport. Twenty-five years later, mountain biking has grown into one of the most popular sports in the world.

These days, mountain biking has become specialized into different disciplines; "cross-country" is climbing and descending at speed on a steep dirt path, "free-ride" is just having fun off-road taking on the biggest drops you dare, while downhill mountain bikes are great big, heavy, full-suspension monsters designed to go down very steep and rocky hillsides as fast as possible.

Mountain biking is a sport that does not depend on competition; it is a great way to enjoy the countryside while flying along a dirt track with a group of friends. It keeps you fit but also requires skill and is a test of nerve, as you learn to take on increasingly difficult descents.

To get started, there are many mountain bike clubs, often run from a local bicycle shop. Inquire there to find out what's in your area.

Road biking

The world's most famous bicycle race, the Tour de France, is the pinnacle of road biking as a sport, but there are many road-biking clubs all over the country that cater to all levels of skill and speed.

A large group will ride together in a pack called the peloton. Riding closely behind another rider reduces the air resistance, so swapping places at the front of the group allows all the riders to go faster for longer. A weekend ride in an amateur club will often be characterized by the less fit riders dropping out of the group until only a few remain, the object being to stay with the pack as long as you can. Clubs are often based from local bicycle shops. For more information you can inquire at your local bicycle shop or visit the "Ride Resources" section on the League of American Bicyclists Web site and enter your state and zip code to find out more about road biking in your area.

Bicycle vacations

Taking a bicycle with you on vacation is one of the best ways to enjoy a new place. It provides excellent mobility in a city, so you can easily find a hotel, and it gives you the option to ride between towns, which means you get to experience the countryside rather than just whiz past it in a car or bus or on a train. It is also a great way to discover remote beaches, villages, or forests often missed by people traveling in faster modes of transportation.

If you prefer to travel in a group, then there are many travel companies that offer organized bike tours to destinations all over the world. There is something for everyone, including many

specialized tours for mountain and road bikers. The advantage of going on an organized tour is that you don't need to carry your own luggage and equipment, which is ferried to the next hotel for you, and if you get tired or break down, a van following the group will pick you up or the group leader will help fix your bike. A professional tour company will also ensure the route is along beautiful, safe routes and is graded for different fitness levels.

If you are happy to carry your own luggage in panniers, and have a competent mechanic in the group, then it is just as easy to organize your own adventure. A week-long trip in a small group without a fixed itinerary, riding between villages, staying in guesthouses and hotels, jumping on the train or bus for some less interesting sections, can be a very pleasant vacation. Try to ensure that there are at least two riders of similar fitness in each group; always waiting for one rider is not fun for anyone, while if there are at least two stronger and two weaker riders it is much less of a problem.

If you are very adventurous, then you can try a full-blown bicycle adventure, whether in the United States or more far-flung places. If you carry a tent and camping stove you can pretty much go anywhere. For more information on bicycle tours see www.bicycleadventures.com (for the western U.S., Canada, and New Zealand); www.adventurecycling.org (for all areas of the U.S.); www.inorbitt.com (for Asian destinations); www.bikeforall.com (for Europe, Asia, Africa, and South America); and www.bicyclingworld.com, which bills itself as the "world's largest collection of bicycle tours."

Extreme cycle sport

Bicycle Moto-Cross (BMX) arrived on the scene in the 1970s and is still very popular with teenagers now, as well as with those who were teenagers in the 1970s and 80s. These strong, small-wheeled machines are used to make jumps either on dirt or in skateboarding parks. It is extremely exciting, and equally difficult and dangerous. If you are already in your thirties or more then it is not recommended that you start to learn now. Twelve- and thirteen-year-olds seem to have a lot more nerve than most thirty- or forty-year-olds.

Trials biking is a form of bicycle acrobatics, balancing generally on one wheel, either front or back, and jumping up onto rocks, fences, and down off roofs. It takes a lot of practice to gain the techniques to balance and make the jumps; as the main skill is balance, it could be started in middle age if you had several hours a day to practice over a period of years. The basic trials-biking technique is the track stand, which involves balancing on two wheels when stopped without putting your feet down. You can practice this while waiting at traffic lights.

Triathlon and iron man competitions include long sections of biking, as well as running and swimming. You will need to be at the peak of physical fitness to compete in one of these, as it is usually harder than running a marathon.

Biking to stores

On weekends, going into town by bike will save you the bus fare or the parking charges, and if you have panniers you can carry quite a lot home if you go shopping. A bicycle is ideal for going down to the corner store to pick up a paper, some bread or milk, or a bottle of wine.

Help give kids their freedom

Children can't drive. With more and more cars on the streets, some of our suburbs have become dangerous places for kids to play. Surveys show that most children want to cycle to school—at one of the most congested times of the day.

You can help to change this by raising awareness at your child's school and organizing a biking-to-school campaign. Of course, the routes must be safe and season conducive.

Biking with your children, or encouraging them to bike to school and get the training they need to keep them safe, will keep them fit and give them freedom and independence to get around without an adult.

Biking with children

Make sure your child has a high-visibility jacket or vest and wears a helmet that fits (it should be firm on the head without discomfort), and that there are lights on the bike. Give the bike a maintenance check, make sure that the brakes work, and that there are no strange noises when your child rides.

If you have young children, you can carry them on a child seat fixed to the back of your bike or on a crossbar child seat. You can also get child trailers, which you strap the child into and tow behind your bike. Plan a safe route that follows quiet roads—if possible, try it out with your child at a quiet time of day.

Chapter 9

FURTHER INFORMATION

If you are looking for cycling companions, maps, training, group rides, and events, or help with getting your bike fixed, there are many places where you can get support and advice:

Adventure Cycling Association An organization that is an all-around cycling resource that creates maps for personalized tours and is working with other organizations to develop the National Bicycle Route Network. **www.adventurecycling.org**. They publish *Adventure Cyclist* magazine and *The Cyclists' Yellow Pages*.

Bike Collective Network Aims to strengthen and encourage communication and resource sharing between existing and future community bike shops. Their Web site directory and wiki include links to scores of bike collectives, bike shops, and pro-bicycling organizations around the world. **www.bikecollectives.org**.

Bike-to-Work Week A nationally coordinated week of events in many states, cities, and town, to promote cycling nationwide. It usually happens the third week of May. See the LAB Web site **www.bikeleague.org**.

Car-Free Day (September 22) Once a year, as part of a world-wide initiative, people everywhere are asked to leave their cars at home and travel more sustainably. The day is often characterized by a series of events organized to promote sustainable travel. One of the most popular events is the car-free festival, where a road is closed to traffic for a day to allow the local community to enjoy activities like slow bicycle races, fancy dress competitions, and sometimes bands and entertainment.

Often the local transportation authority will provide free public transport for one day, car clubs will give free membership, and there will be free bicycle checks and secure bicycle parking.

While the single Car-Free Day is a largely European phenomenon (see www.worldcarfree.net) that has yet to catch on in the United States, an Internet search shows that Curb-Your-Car months and (CYC coalitions) are springing up in many places, from Vermont and New Hampshire to Utah, from Michigan to Texas.

Critical Mass started in San Francisco as a monthly ride for cyclists to get together and ride en masse around the city, so that for once cyclists would be the majority of traffic. The concept went global, and now there are regular masses in most major cities worldwide. The popular slogan associated with the movement is: "We're not blocking traffic, we are traffic."

Critical Mass rides often take place on the last Friday of the month. More information and a comprehensive listing of the rides and related events in cities across the country can be found at http://critical-mass.info/.

League of American Bicyclists (LAB) is a national organization that advocates for bicycling and bicyclists. A copy of their National Bike Month Event Organizer's Kit can be obtained through their Web site at www.bikeleague.org.

National Bicycle Route Network Still in its planning phase, this network of bike paths and bike trails will stretch from coast to coast. http://adventurecycling.org/routes/index.cfm.

National Bike Month May is National Bike Month, which includes Bike-to-Work Week. Find out more at the Web site of the League of American Bicyclists (LAB) www.bikeleague.org.

The Pedestrian and Bicycle Information Center is a resource for all aspects of nonmotorized transportation. Their Web site is at www.bicyclinginfo.org.

She Cycles A British Web site with forums and tips for women cyclists. www.shecycles.com.

Winter Riding For tips about riding your bicycle in winter, check out the Icebike Web site at www.icebike.com.

Here's a small selection of organizations in Canada, listed by province, that promote bicycling as a sensible form of transportation and offer support to or advocacy for bikers.

Alberta
  Edmonton Bicycle Commuters' Society,
  www.edmontonbikes.ca.

British Columbia
  PEDAL—Pedal Energy Development Alternatives
  (Vancouver), www.pedalpower.org.

  Victoria Transport Institute, www.vtpi.org.

Ontario
  Cycle Ontario Alliance / Ontario en Vélo,
  www.cycleontario.ca.

  Citizens for Safe Cycling (Ottawa), www.safecycling.ca.

  Community Bicycle Network (Toronto),
  www.communitybicyclenetwork.org.

Québec
  Right to Move / La Voie Libre (Montréal), www.rtm-lvl.org.

Index

green press INITIATIVE

Chelsea Green Publishing Company is committed to preserving ancient forests and natural resources. We elected to print *Biking to Work* on 100% postconsumer recycled paper, processed chlorine-free. As a result, for this printing, using 2,772 pounds of Silva Enviro100 text stock instead of virgin-fibers paper, we have saved:

24 trees
1,497 pounds of solid waste
14,132 gallons of water
9.5 pounds of contaminants suspended
in the water
3,288 pounds of greenhouse-gas air emissions
3,426 cubic feet of natural gas

Chelsea Green Publishing made this paper choice because we are a member of the Green Press Initiative, a nonprofit program dedicated to supporting authors, publishers, and suppliers in their efforts to reduce their use of fiber obtained from endangered forests. For more information, visit www.greenpressinitiative.org.

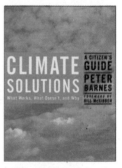